GW00706077

Daughter

Daughter

$\mathcal{A}$ daughter . . .

more attractive and precious

than are jewels.

—SONGS OF MILAREPA

Someone would like to have

you for her child but

you are mine.

—AKAN VERSE

She can teach ye how to climb

Higher than the sphery chime . . .

—JOHN MILTON

Daughter

Illustrated by
Stephanie Dalton Cowan

ARIEL BOOKS

Andrews McMeel
Publishing
Kansas City

For information write Andrews McMeel
Publishing, an Andrews McMeel
Universal company, 4520 Main Street,
Kansas City, Missouri 64111.

Illustrations copyright © 2002 by
Stephanie Dalton Cowan
Edited by Margaret Lannamann

ISBN: 0-7407-2280-8
Library of Congress Catalog Card Number:
2001096362

To my daughter Leonora

without whose never-failing

sympathy and encouragement

this book would have been

finished in half the time.

—P. G. WODEHOUSE

I too am a rare

Pattern.

—Amy Lowell

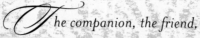*The companion, the friend,*
and confidante of her mother . . .

—RICHARD STEELE

You see, our children are

indispensable to us . . .

this child whom we love brings

daylight into our soul and

into our home.

—VICTOR HUGO

Of all nature's gifts to

the human race, what is sweeter

to a man than his children?

—CICERO

When a girl is born,

it's a good omen for the family.

—JEWISH PROVERB

"Flowers of the home,"

says he,

"Are daughters."

—MARCELINE DESBORDES-VALMORE

They are idols
of hearts and of households;
They are angels of God
in disguise;
The sunlight still sleeps
in their tresses,
His glory still gleams in their eyes.

—CHARLES DICKENS

NOTES

Aisha al-Taimuriya (1840–1902), "Embroidered Ornaments"

Akan verse (dates unknown), "Lullaby"

Alcott, Louisa May (1832–1888), *Little Women*, 1868 (p. 62)

Anonymous song (12th–13th century)

Aretino, Pietro (1492–1557), "Letter to Sebastiano the painter, brother of Piombo, of the baptism of his own little daughter, Adria"

Astell, Mary (1666–1731), "A Serious Proposal to the Ladies"

Beauvoir, Simone de (1908–1986), *The Second Sex*, 1949

Bierce, Ambrose (1842–c. 1914), "Rosalie"

Bradstreet, Anne (1612–1672), "The Tenth Muse, Lately Sprung Up in America," 1650

Brontë, Emily (1818–1848) or Charlotte Brontë (1816–1855), *Stanzas*

Brontë, Emily (1818–1848), *Last Lines*, 1846

Brooks, Shirley (1816–1874), "The Philosopher and Her Father"

Brown, John Gregory, *Decorations in a Ruined Cemetery*, 1994

Browning, Elizabeth Barrett (1806–1861), "The House of Clouds" (p. 88); "Isobel's Child" (p. 9)

Bryant, William Cullen (1794–1878), "Lines on Revisiting the Country"

Burns, Robert (1759–1796), "Bonnie Lesley"

Cicero (106–43 B.C.), *Post Reditum ad Quirites*

Clarke, Austin (1896–1974), *The Planter's Daughter*, 1929

Cowper, William (1731–1800), "To a Young Lady"

Dafydd ap Gwilym (14th century), *"Yr Wylan"*

Desbordes-Valmore, Marceline (1786–1859), *Idyls*

Dickens, Charles (1812–1870), "The Children"

Droste-Hülshoff, Annette von (1797–1848), "On the Tower"

Euripides (c. 484–406 B.C.), *The Suppliant Women*

Fuller, Margaret (1810–1850), "Letter to Emerson," 1838

Gordon, George, Lord Byron (1788–1824), *Childe Harold*

Greene, Graham (1904–1991), *The Power and the Glory*, 1940

Onkinerah, David (dates unknown), "Bliss"

Parnell, Thomas (1679–1718), "Song," 1714

Philips, Ambrose (1674–1749), "To Charlotte Pulteney"

Philips, Katherine (1631–1664), "To My Excellent
    Lucasia, on Our Friendship"

Ransom, John Crowe (1888–1974), "Bells for John
    Whiteside's Daughter," 1924

Reik, Theodor (20th century)

Rinehart, Mary Roberts (1876–1958), "The Family
    Friend," *Affinities*, 1920

Ruskin, John (1819–1900), *Sesame and Lilies*, 1865

Saitoti, Tepilit Ole (1949–), *The Worlds of a Maasai
    Warrior*, 1986

Sangster, Margaret E. (1838–1912), *The Art of Home
    Making*, 1898

Scholasticus, Agathias (dates unknown)

Scott, Sir Walter (1771–1832), *Rokeby*

Segea, Luisa (1522–1560), *Dialogue of Blesilla and Flaminia*

Shakespeare, William (1564–1616), *The Sonnets*
    (p. 19); *Twelfth-Night*, 1598–1600 (p. 77)

Shelley, Mary (1797–1851), *Frankenstein*

. . . between mothers
and daughters there is a kind
of blood-hyphen
that is, finally, indissoluble.

—CAROL SHIELDS

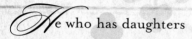

He who has daughters
is always a shepherd.

—SPANISH PROVERB

He had one son and many daughters.

His love for his daughters was

unmatched . . .

—TEPILIT OLE SAITOTI

I have lived in liberty,

I have spun with abandon

across open floors

to the music of fiddles,

I have slept, I have woken

to a dawn song of pipes.

—MÁIRI MACLEOD

Many years have passed,

but not her girlish laughter . . .

—Agathias Scholasticus

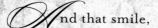And that smile,

     like sunshine, dart

Into many a sunless heart,

For a smile of God thou art.

—HENRY WADSWORTH LONGFELLOW

I myself am more divine
than any I see.

—MARGARET FULLER

I am strong in the spirit,—
deep-thoughted, clear-eyed.

—ELIZABETH BARRETT BROWNING

My days have been so
wondrous free,
The little birds that fly
With careless ease
from tree to tree,
Were but as blessed as I.

—THOMAS PARNELL

All things

Crowd me in!

I am so wide!

—Hadewijch of Antwerp

. . . this dynastic awareness of time, this shared belonging to a chain of generations . . . we collaborate together to root each other in a dimension of time longer than our own lives.

—MICHAEL IGNATIEFF

 *She grows*

as a flower does.

—JOHN RUSKIN

There is always one moment

in childhood when the door

opens and lets the future in.

—GRAHAM GREENE

Le

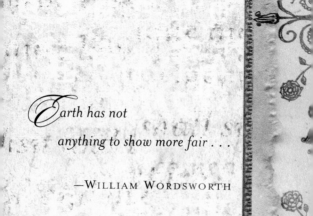

Earth has not

anything to show more fair . . .

—WILLIAM WORDSWORTH

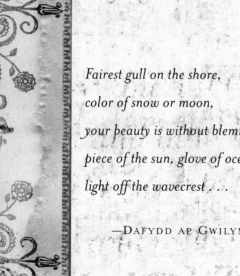

Fairest gull on the shore,

color of snow or moon,

your beauty is without blemish—

piece of the sun, glove of ocean,

light off the wavecrest . . .

—DAFYDD AP GWILYM

Ah, lucky girls who
grow up in the shelter
of a mother's love.

—EDITH WHARTON

And O!

She was the Sunday

In every week.

—AUSTIN CLARKE

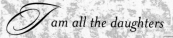 I am all the daughters
of my father's house . . .

—WILLIAM SHAKESPEARE

*S*he discovered with great
delight that one does not love
one's children just because they
are one's children but because
of the friendship formed
while raising them.

—GABRIEL GARCÍA MÁRQUEZ

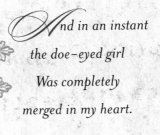

And in an instant

the doe-eyed girl

Was completely

merged in my heart.

—MARULA

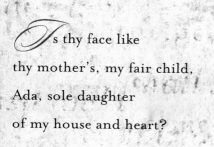

*I*s thy face like
thy mother's, my fair child,
Ada, sole daughter
of my house and heart?

—GEORGE GORDON, LORD BYRON

. . . a very delicate bond
of sympathy and friendship

between the father

and his daughter.

—MARGARET E. SANGSTER

For I have taught her,

with delighted eye,

To gaze upon the mountains,—

to behold,

With deep affection,

the pure ample sky . . .

—WILLIAM CULLEN BRYANT

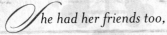

She had her friends too,

blithe young girls,

Who whispered, babbled, laughed, caressed,

And romped and danced with dancing curls,

And gave our life a joyous zest.

—JAMES THOMSON

$\mathcal{A}$nd sweet 'twas to see their

light footsteps advance

Like the wing of the breeze

through the maze

of the dance.

—LYDIA HOWARD SIGOURNEY

Lithesome, blithesome daughter mine . . .

Greet me with those eyes of blue,

Eyes which seem to look me through . . .

—AMBROSE BIERCE

. . . the young wonder-tree.

—BARONGA FOLK TALE

For thou art

all that I can prize . . .

—KATHERINE PHILIPS

Mothers raise their daughters

and let

their sons grow up.

—AFRICAN-AMERICAN PROVERB

. . . Mother and Child . . . indelible
and indestructible—the strongest
bond upon this earth.

—THEODOR REIK

I'd rather see you poor men's wives,

if you were happy, beloved, contented,

than queens on thrones,

without self-respect and peace.

—LOUISA MAY ALCOTT

. . . *such speed in her little body,*

And such lightness in her footfall.

—JOHN CROWE RANSOM

To an old father,

nothing is more sweet

Than a daughter.

—EURIPIDES

There's something like a line of gold thread running through a man's words when he talks to his daughter, and gradually over the years it gets to be long enough for you to pick up in your hands and weave into a cloth that feels like love itself.

—JOHN GREGORY BROWN

When she laughs,

there's no one like her;

When she sulks, she's more lovely

than before.

—SHEN YÜEH

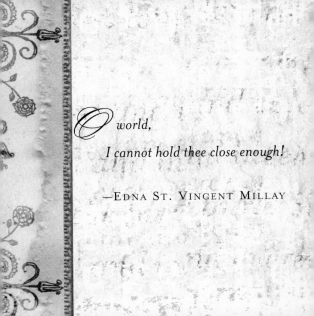

$\mathcal{O}$ world,

I cannot hold thee close enough!

—EDNA ST. VINCENT MILLAY

. . . she has visions and strange dreams,

And in all her words and ways, she seems

Much older than she is in truth.

Who would think her but fifteen?

—HENRY WADSWORTH LONGFELLOW

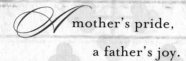

A mother's pride,

a father's joy.

—SIR WALTER SCOTT

Love, sweetness, goodness,

in her person shined

So clear, as in no face

with more delight.

—JOHN MILTON

That experience must be extraordinary—for a woman to have a daughter and really see another woman, part image of herself.

—GLORIA VANDERBILT

The shadow of my mother

danced . . . to a tune that

my shadow sang.

—JAMAICA KINCAID

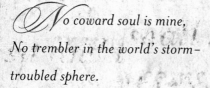

No coward soul is mine,
No trembler in the world's storm-
troubled sphere.

—EMILY BRONTË

My dreams were all my own;

I accounted for them to nobody;

They were my refuge when annoyed—

my dearest pleasure when free.

—MARY SHELLEY

Le

. . . childish thoughts,

like flowers, would drift away . . .

—JEAN INGELOW

From her cradle . . .

her only delight

Was in breaking

commandments from

morning till night.

—GEORGE DU MAURIER

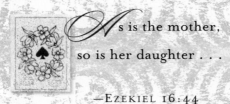 s is the mother,

so is her daughter . . .

—EZEKIEL 16:44

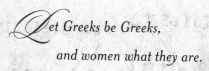

Let Greeks be Greeks,

and women what they are.

—ANNE BRADSTREET

Many daughters have

done virtuously,

but thou excellest them all.

—PROVERBS 31:29

. . . my child, my child . . .

Sweet image of your sire!

—SHIRLEY BROOKS

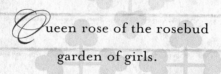

Queen rose of the rosebud
garden of girls.

—ALFRED, LORD TENNYSON

Blaze with the fire that
is never extinguished.

—LUISA SEGEA

All that is required of you,
is only to be as happy as possibly
you can, and to make sure of
a felicity that will fill all
the capacities of your souls!

—MARY ASTELL

We possess nothing in the world—

except the power to say "I."

—SIMONE WEIL

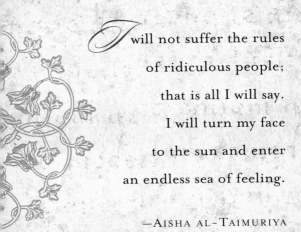

I will not suffer the rules
of ridiculous people;
that is all I will say.
I will turn my face
to the sun and enter
an endless sea of feeling.

—AISHA AL-TAIMURIYA

Womanly grace

and child-like innocence . . .

—JOHN GREENLEAF WHITTIER

$\mathcal{O}$nly take this rule along,

Always to advise her wrong;

And reprove her when she's right;

She may then grow wise for spite.

—JONATHAN SWIFT

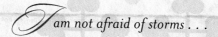

I am not afraid of storms . . .

—LOUISA MAY ALCOTT

$\mathcal{I}$ am a young girl, gay,

graceful, not yet

in my fifteenth year. . . .

I should be set

for love and hear

its lovely bell.

—ANONYMOUS SONG

A rosebud set

with little willful thorns.

—ALFRED, LORD TENNYSON

She has no need . . . of the sun—

she has her own radiance.

—JUDAH HALEVI

. . . nor does an hour pass

in which her parents

do not rejoice

in her lovableness . . .

—PIETRO ARETINO

*W*hen she laughs,

we will burst into song . . .

—DAVID ONKINERAH

She shall be sportive as the fawn

That wild with glee across the lawn . . .

—WILLIAM WORDSWORTH

Heaven reflected in her face . . .

—WILLIAM COWPER

. . . for the mother at once

her double and another person.

—SIMONE DE BEAUVOIR

imely blossom, Infant fair,
Fondling of a happy pair . . .

—AMBROSE PHILIPS

Thou art thy mother's glass,
and she in thee
Calls back the lovely April
of her prime . . .

—WILLIAM SHAKESPEARE

Theophilis,

daughter of Cleocha,

made it—daughter,

mother, grandmother

woven in the thread.

—NOSSIS

To see her is to love her . . .

For Nature made her what she is,

And ne'er made sic anither!

—ROBERT BURNS

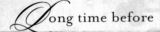

Long time before
I in my mother's womb was born,
    A God, preparing,
        did this glorious store,
    The world, for me adorn . . .

                —THOMAS TRAHERNE